PHOENIX SUNS

ALL-TIME GREATS

BY TED COLEMAN

Book design by Jake Slavik
Cover design by Jake Slavik

Photographs ©: Charles Rex Arbogast/AP Images, cover (top), 1 (top); Al Messerschmidt/AP Images, cover (bottom), 1 (bottom); Robert Kradin/AP Images, 4; Fred Jewell/AP Images, 6; Walter J. Zeboski/AP Images, 9; Mark Elias/AP Images, 10; Jeff Kida/AP Images, 12; Bill Chan/AP Images, 15; Mark J. Terrill/AP Images, 16; Paul Connors/AP Images, 19; Matt York/AP Images, 20

Press Box Books, an imprint of Press Room Editions.

ISBN
978-1-63494-605-6 (library bound)
978-1-63494-623-0 (paperback)
978-1-63494-641-4 (epub)
978-1-63494-657-5 (hosted ebook)

Library of Congress Control Number: 2022913243

Distributed by North Star Editions, Inc.
2297 Waters Drive
Mendota Heights, MN 55120
www.northstareditions.com

Printed in the United States of America
Mankato, MN
012023

ABOUT THE AUTHOR

Ted Coleman is a freelance sportswriter and children's book author who lives in Louisville, Kentucky, with his trusty Affenpinscher, Chloe.

TABLE OF CONTENTS

CHAPTER 1

NBA SUNRISE 4

CHAPTER 2

HOT AS EVER 10

CHAPTER 3

RUNNING POINT 16

TIMELINE 22

TEAM FACTS 23

MORE INFORMATION 23

GLOSSARY 24

INDEX 24

HAWKINS
42

CHAPTER 1
NBA SUNRISE

There's a reason **Dick Van Arsdale** is called "The Original Sun." The guard was the team's first pick in the 1968 expansion draft. And on October 18, 1968, he scored the team's first basket. Van Arsdale played nine years for the Suns. He later worked for the team for decades.

Another scoring option during those early years was **Connie Hawkins**. "Hawk" was an amazing athlete. The forward was one of the first players known for high-flying play. He led

the Suns in scoring as they made their first playoff appearance in 1970.

Running the Suns offense was **Charlie Scott**. The playmaking point guard averaged more than 24 points per game in Phoenix. But the Suns struggled to get back to the playoffs.

That changed in 1975–76. Center **Alvan Adams** was the NBA Rookie of the Year. He was a fierce rebounder and scorer. **Paul Westphal** made an even bigger impact. The guard helped transform the Suns' offense. Westphal was known for how he thought through the game. That helped him consistently set up his teammates.

The Suns went just 42–40 in 1975–76. But Westphal led the Suns all the way to the NBA Finals. That series featured a triple-overtime classic in Game 5. The Suns

JERRY COLANGELO

Nobody has had more of an impact on the Suns than Jerry Colangelo. He was the team's first general manager. He then served as head coach in the 1970s. Colangelo held many other jobs with the team and even became its owner. In all, Colangelo worked for the Suns for 43 years. He also led the US Olympic men's basketball teams for many years.

lost 128–126. It went on to be known as "The Greatest Game Ever Played."

The Suns had another Rookie of the Year in 1978. Swingman **Walter Davis** regularly scored at least 20 points per game. Davis made six All-Star teams with the Suns. He also led a conference finals appearance in 1979.

Adams, Davis, and **Larry Nance** were key Suns in the 1980s. Nance was one of the greatest dunk artists of the 1980s. He won the Slam Dunk Contest in 1984. Phoenix made it back to the conference finals that year. However, the Suns had to wait a bit for their next trip.

STAT SPOTLIGHT

CAREER POINTS

SUNS TEAM RECORD

Walter Davis: 15,666

PHOENIX
SUNS
Kings
DAVIS
6

SUNS
7
BULLS
21
JOHNSON
7

CHAPTER 2

HOT AS EVER

The Suns' older core began to dissolve in the late 1980s. A new generation led by point guard **Kevin Johnson** eventually took over. "KJ" helped turn the Suns around. He was the playmaker the team needed. Johnson played 12 seasons in Phoenix. The Suns made the playoffs in all but one of them.

Center **Mark West** gave the Suns a presence under the basket. West didn't shoot much. But when he did, he rarely missed. He led the NBA in making 62.5 percent of his shots in 1989–90.

PHOENIX
24
SUNS
CHAMBERS
24

The Suns' playoff hopes got a big boost when they signed forward **Tom Chambers** in 1988. Chambers was one of the best scorers of his era. He averaged more than 20 points per game in his time in Phoenix.

Also coming to the team in 1988 was swingman **Dan Majerle**. "Thunder Dan" was a great shooter from distance. But he was known for his defense. Majerle twice made the NBA All-Defensive Second Team.

One of Majerle's backcourt partners was **Jeff Hornacek**. The guard was the team's third scoring option behind Johnson and Chambers. He was a skilled playmaker and

STAT SPOTLIGHT

POINTS PER GAME

SUNS TEAM RECORD

Tom Chambers: 27.2 (1989–90)

good shooter. The Suns made runs to the conference finals in 1989 and 1990.

Hornacek was part of the biggest trade in Suns history. In 1992, he was sent with two players to the Philadelphia 76ers. Forward **Charles Barkley** headed to Phoenix. Barkley averaged more than 20 points and 10 rebounds in all four seasons in Phoenix. The Hall of Famer instantly made the Suns a championship contender.

The 1992–93 Suns won a team-record 62 games. Barkley was the league's Most Valuable Player (MVP).

COACH FITZSIMMONS

Cotton Fitzsimmons first coached the Suns in the early 1970s. He returned in 1988 and helped lead the best era in team history. By 1992–93, he was working in the team's front office. He was the key builder of the 1993 NBA Finals team. Fitzsimmons later returned to the bench as coach in the mid-90s. In total, Fitzsimmons was one of the most successful Suns coaches.

He averaged 25.6 points and 12.2 rebounds per game. The Suns pushed Michael Jordan and the Chicago Bulls to six games in the NBA Finals. Though they lost a heartbreaking Game 6 at home, the Suns still had their best season ever.

KIDD
32

CHAPTER 3

RUNNING POINT

The Suns with Charles Barkley remained one of the best teams in the NBA. But he was gone after the 1995–96 season. Most of the 1992–93 team was gone by then, too. But that year, point guard **Jason Kidd** arrived.

Kidd had been an All-Star for the Dallas Mavericks. He shined for the Suns as one of the league's best playmakers. He led the league in assists for three straight seasons in Phoenix.

One of Kidd's top weapons was forward **Shawn Marion**. Marion was never quite a superstar. But he was a consistently solid all-around player for the Suns. He was a four-time All-Star.

In 2002, the Suns added another forward in **Amar'e Stoudemire**. Like Marion, Stoudemire was super athletic. He was also an elite scorer and rebounder. Stoudemire formed a dynamic duo with new point guard **Steve Nash**.

Earlier, Nash and Kidd had been teammates. But Nash was traded to Dallas in favor of Kidd in the 1990s. Nash returned in 2004 and led the explosive Phoenix offense. The Suns tried to shoot the ball seven seconds or less into each possession. That led to them leading the

STAT SPOTLIGHT

CAREER ASSISTS

SUNS TEAM RECORD

Steve Nash: 6,997

NASH
13

league in scoring five times while Nash ran the offense.

Nash was an amazing passer and playmaker. He won two MVPs in a Suns uniform. And he led Phoenix to three conference finals appearances.

That core never made the Finals, however. By 2015 the Suns had a losing record. But that year they drafted guard **Devin Booker**. Booker soon turned into one of the NBA's best offensive players. "Book" could score from anywhere. And he did it in bunches. Booker scored 70 points in a game in March 2017.

At point guard, the Suns traded for **Chris Paul** in 2020. Booker and Paul formed another dynamic duo. They led the Suns back to the NBA Finals in 2021. Although they lost, fans had hope another great Suns team was on the rise.

AL MCCOY

Al McCoy was not the first broadcaster in Suns history. But it's hard to remember anyone else. The 2021–22 season was McCoy's 50th as the voice of the Suns. That was a record for an NBA broadcaster with one team. That same year, he turned 89. On his birthday, he called a Suns playoff game.

TIMELINE

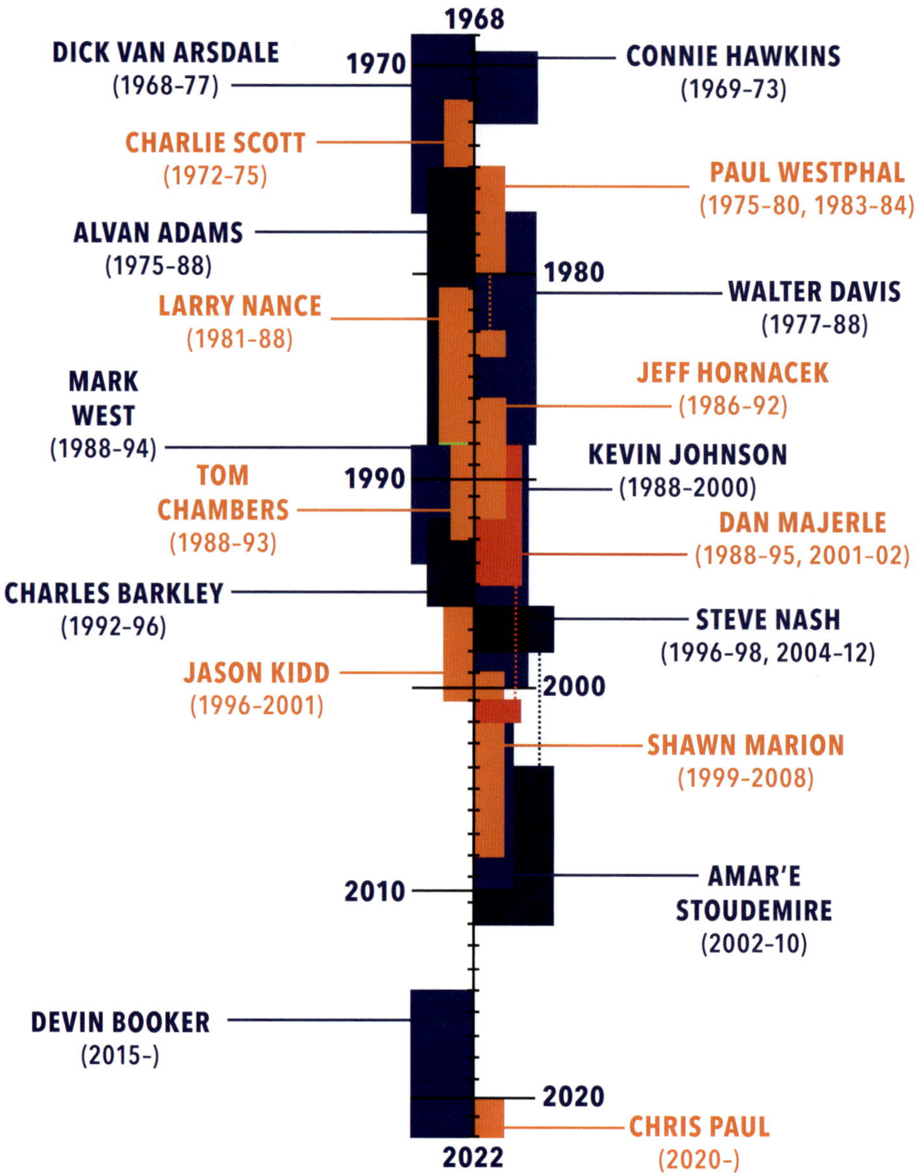

1968
DICK VAN ARSDALE (1968-77)
1970
CONNIE HAWKINS (1969-73)
CHARLIE SCOTT (1972-75)
PAUL WESTPHAL (1975-80, 1983-84)
ALVAN ADAMS (1975-88)
1980
WALTER DAVIS (1977-88)
LARRY NANCE (1981-88)
JEFF HORNACEK (1986-92)
MARK WEST (1988-94)
KEVIN JOHNSON (1988-2000)
1990
TOM CHAMBERS (1988-93)
DAN MAJERLE (1988-95, 2001-02)
CHARLES BARKLEY (1992-96)
STEVE NASH (1996-98, 2004-12)
JASON KIDD (1996-2001)
2000
SHAWN MARION (1999-2008)
2010
AMAR'E STOUDEMIRE (2002-10)
DEVIN BOOKER (2015-)
2020
CHRIS PAUL (2020-)
2022

TEAM FACTS

PHOENIX SUNS

First Season: 1968–69

NBA titles: 0*

Key coaches:

Mike D'Antoni (2003–04 to 2007–08)
253–136, 26–25 playoffs

John MacLeod (1973–74 to 1986–87)
579–543, 37–44 playoffs

Paul Westphal (1992–93 to 1995–96)
191–88, 25–19 playoffs

MORE INFORMATION

To learn more about the Phoenix Suns, go to **pressboxbooks.com/AllAccess.**

These links are routinely monitored and updated to provide the most current information available.

**Through 2021–22 season*

GLOSSARY

contender
A team that is good enough to win a title.

draft
A system that allows teams to acquire new players coming into a league.

dynamic
Energetic, creating positive change.

elite
The best of the best.

expansion
The way leagues grow by adding new teams.

overtime
An additional period of play to decide a game's winner.

rookie
A first-year player.

swingman
A player who can play both guard and forward.

INDEX

Adams, Alvan, 7–8

Barkley, Charles, 14, 17
Booker, Devin, 21

Chambers, Tom, 13
Colangelo, Jerry, 7

Davis, Walter, 8

Fitzsimmons, Cotton, 14

Hawkins, Connie, 5
Hornacek, Jeff, 13–14

Johnson, Kevin, 11, 13
Jordan, Michael, 15

Kidd, Jason, 17–18

Majerle, Dan, 13
Marion, Shawn, 17–18
McCoy, Al, 21

Nance, Larry, 8
Nash, Steve, 18, 20

Paul, Chris, 21

Scott, Charlie, 6
Stoudemire, Amar'e, 18

Van Arsdale, Dick, 5

West, Mark, 11
Westphal, Paul, 7